SOLA

SOLA

Mark Hallock & Ben Haley

CONTENTS

FOREWORD

At the heart of the Reformation lay five basic principles which, if not explicitly listed as such, have for future generations come to epitomize the distinctive contribution of Protestantism to the church's faith: faith alone, scripture alone, grace alone, Christ alone, and the glory of God alone. The reformers of course believed more than just these five things and shared much in common with the Roman Catholic Church: the Trinity, for example. But these five solas, five 'alones', captured biblical teaching which they thought had either been neglected or even rejected by the medieval church.

Today the church faces some interesting challenges. A rampant secularism presses in from wider society, demanding that the church conform to its standards on matters such as sexuality and abortion. Internally, the church is challenged not simply by those who are tempted to succumb to the pressure of the world but also by those who simply do not understand the gospel. Both can be disturbing but neither need be particularly worrying. The church of Paul's day faced very similar external and internal dangers and yet survived.

Yet the question of strategy then comes to the fore: How did Paul handle these problems?   The answer is simple: He called upon the churches to whom he wrote to understand who they were, to act in accordance with who they were, and therefore to be who they were. And he did that by expounding to them again and again the basics of the gospel.

To be a Protestant Christian is to believe that Paul was correct. It is to see that teaching the gospel to Christians is the most important thing the church can do. And it is therefore to press upon congregations and upon individuals the importance of those five basic pillars of Reformation theology, the solas.

You could fill a library with the learned tomes written on each of these topics. But here, in this book, you have a fine and clear summary of the essential point of each of them. This little volume is both a good place for the new Christian to start and a concise reminder to the veteran Christian of some of the most important things there are to know about the faith.

Carl R. Trueman
Grove City College,
August 2018.

INTRODUCTION

If you were to visit the city of Wittenberg, Germany, today, you would find that Christianity there is essentially dead. It is a sad testament to the decline of the Christian faith in Europe. But 500 years ago, the religious landscape was much different. In those days, the Roman Catholic Church was alive and well.

A certain monk lived in Wittenberg in those days, having entered the monastery after a lightning strike during a thunderstorm had terrified him so profoundly that he vowed he would serve God if only he could survive the storm. He was teaching as a professor, and at thirty-four years of age, he began to publish theological writings. A most significant detail about this particular monk is that at this time he was unconverted.

It was a time of deep spiritual unrest for the monk. Eventually, his spiritual wrestling and study of the Scriptures led to his conversion. He began to take issue with several aspects of the Roman Catholic Church in which he served, and 500 years ago the monk nailed his Ninety-Five Theses to the door of the Castle Church in Wittenberg—a place you can still visit today. It was October 31, 1517.

The monk of course was Martin Luther, and with that one act he explosively ignited the Protestant Reformation. It was an event that quite literally changed the course of human history. What was to take place in the years to come not only profoundly altered the religious landscape of Europe, but in many ways it is the very reason that we gather as Protestants week in and week out in our churches.

Our forefathers in the faith, men like Martin Luther, protested what they saw as biblical and theological errors in the Roman Catholic Church. The doctrines that the Reformers—so named because they had as their goal the *reformation* of the church—the doctrines that they proclaimed were not new doctrines; in fact, they were actually very old doctrines. The Reformers stood squarely in a stream of history that flowed back through the ages to the church fathers and then beyond them to the apostles and Christ Himself. As Protestant Christians today, we stand in that very same stream; our own roots can be traced back to that fateful day in Wittenberg, Germany, 500 years ago.

As Protestant Christians today, we stand in that very same stream; our own roots can be traced back to that fateful day in Wittenberg, Germany, 500 years ago.

The purpose of this book is to define—and rejoice in—five core doctrines that have come to be identified as the pillars of the Protestant Reformation. These doctrines were the resounding battle cry of the Reformers. They are known as the five *Solas*—*sola* being a Latin word that means "alone" or "only."

The fundamental and foundational question of the Reformation that the five Solas sought to address is this:

How can sinful men and women be made right with a holy God? In other words, how can broken, messed up, sinful individuals like us be saved? That was the burning question of Martin Luther and the other Reformers. This was the heart of the Reformation.

The five *Solas* summarize the truth of how we are saved from sin and the purpose for which we are saved. They describe in great clarity from the Scriptures how we can know God and experience relationship with Him. These are the doctrines that make us distinctly Protestant Christians. They form the basis upon which our understanding of the gospel stands or falls. These are doctrines that have been fought for and defended for 500 years because within them is the essence of what we consider the Christian gospel. These five doctrines are doctrines for which men and women have been burned at the stake.

If we get these five doctrines wrong, then the gospel of Jesus Christ is obscured. Hidden. Perverted. With that sobering reality in mind, the purpose of this book is not merely an exercise in history. Rather, it is our intention to highlight not only how *glorious*, but also how *practical* these truths are for the Christian life. Properly understood, these doctrines shine the full light of God's glory upon the gospel that we believe. And what is more, they should affect us profoundly in every area of life.

Doctrines like these are not boring or lame. No matter our church background, we want to know God rightly. But this desire for knowledge needs to spring forth from hearts that are set aflame for God and His glory. Our hope in

If we get these five doctrines wrong, then the gospel of Jesus Christ is obscured.

writing this book is that these doctrines would ignite a reformation—a revival—in your own soul as you are reminded again of these precious truths. As we come to a fuller understanding of how these doctrines give us peace and assurance and hope and joy, may these magnificent truths from God's Word lead us to more full-throated worship: discerned from Scripture Alone, through Faith Alone, by Grace Alone, in Christ Alone, and for the Glory of God Alone.

SOLA SCRIPTURA

(Scripture Alone)

The first of the five *Solas* that we will unpack is *Sola Scriptura*. It simply means *"Scripture Alone."* Let's first look briefly at its meaning. What do we mean when we say *Scripture alone*? It may be helpful at the outset to outline what it *doesn't* mean. It doesn't mean that all we need is the Bible and we should throw away our other books. It doesn't negate the fellowship of the church, or preaching, or seminary classes. It doesn't mean our historical church traditions are meaningless. The reality is that there is much value in all of those things!

The Meaning of Sola Scriptura

Here is what *Sola Scriptura* means at the most basic level. It means that *Scripture alone is the final, sole authority on all spiritual matters.* There is no authority or rule of truth that is equal to or surpasses the Word of God. Church tradition, human philosophy, our own personal experience—while

> *There is no authority or rule of truth that is equal to or surpasses the Word of God.*

these things can be supplemental and helpful in our understanding of salvation, it is the Word of God that ultimately stands alone.

Sola Scriptura means that all things necessary for salvation are taught in the sixty-six books of the Bible. This doctrine goes hand-in-hand with another doctrine called the *perspicuity* of the Scriptures. That's a word that means *clarity*. This should cause us to rejoice! Taken together, Christians believe that the necessary things needed to understand salvation are taught clearly enough in the Scriptures for the ordinary person to read them, understand them, and be saved.

It is important for us in our modern day and age to understand that this doctrine is in direct conflict with the teaching of the Roman Catholic Church. The Catholic Church teaches that Scripture does *not* stand alone. The official teaching from the Second Vatican Council in the 1960s reads this: "It is not from sacred Scripture alone that the church draws her certainty about everything which has been revealed. Therefore, sacred tradition and sacred Scripture are to be accepted and venerated with the same devotion and reverence."[1]

As Protestant Christians we would happily agree that the tradition of the church is incredibly important, full of much good and much truth—but it is not the final authority. It is not to be held at the same level as Scripture. That is the essence of *Sola Scriptura*. The truth in some traditions is good; some traditions are biblical, others are not. But our traditions have to be evaluated in light of the Scriptures. This is true when we consider our differences with Catholicism, but it's also true of our own Protestant traditions! Many of our cherished and celebrated traditions in the church today have less to do with Scripture and more to do with preference.

The truth of the matter is that people err. Traditions err. Popes err. Councils err. But the Word of God does not err. The Word of God is flawless. It is perfect. It is the ultimate authority. It will stand forever. It will never pass away. God has spoken and God cannot lie. His Word is truth. His Word is light. His Word

> *Traditions err. Popes err. Councils err. But the Word of God does not err. The Word of God is flawless.*

is life. That is the doctrine of *Sola Scriptura*, and it was the rallying cry of the Protestant Reformation. May it still be our rallying cry today!

Martin Luther, eventually excommunicated from the Roman Catholic Church, was put on trial as a heretic in Worms, Germany. Asked to renounce his teachings,

Martin Luther stood up and said this: "Unless I am convinced by Scripture and plain reason—I do not accept the authorities of popes and councils because they've contradicted each other—my conscience is captive to the Word of God. I cannot and will not recant anything. For to go against my conscience is neither right nor safe. So help me God. Amen."[2] Martin Luther was bound to the Word of God.

The Westminster Confession of Faith sums up the meaning of *Sola Scriptura* for us when it says this: "The whole council of God, concerning all things necessary for His own glory, man's salvation, faith, and life is either expressly set down in Scripture or by good and necessary consequences may be deduced from Scripture, unto which nothing at any time is to be added whether by new revelations of the Spirit or traditions of men."[3]

> ". . .my conscience is captive to the Word of God."

This is the incredible truth: when the Scripture speaks, God speaks! Have you allowed the weightiness of that to really hit home for you? Our eternal, all-powerful, holy and righteous God, the God who dwells in unapproachable light, the God who knows every molecule in the universe and knows every hair on your head—our God has spoken. To us. To me. To you. When you hold your Bible, you hold

His very words in your hands. If this is true, if God has spoken and Scripture alone is our final authority, then it would follow that we should experience a practical outworking of this truth in our lives.

The Practical Realities of *Sola Scriptura*

Let's now move on to the practical aspects of Sola Scriptura. What does this look like in the Christian life? Does holding this doctrine really affect how we live? There are two main texts we will consider as we answer those questions. The first is found is Acts 17.

#1. We Receive the Word with Eagerness

First, a bit of background. The apostle Paul is on his second missionary journey with his companion Silas. They are traveling from city to city and Paul is reasoning with the Jews about Jesus Christ. Keep in mind that Paul was a preacher. He was the preeminent preacher. And as a preacher, he both taught and reasoned from the Scriptures. Paul loved the Word of God.

He arrives in a town called Berea in Thessalonica; there we meet some Christians who paint for us a vivid picture of what it looks like to trust in the authority and the infallibility of the Scriptures.

Acts 17:10–11 reads, "The brothers immediately sent Paul and Silas away by night to Berea. And when they arrived, they went into the Jewish synagogue. Now these Jews were more noble than those in Thessalonica. They received the word with all eagerness, examining the Scriptures daily to see if these things were so."

There are several things to note in those verses about these Bereans. First of all, note their *posture*. They received the Word with all eagerness. As Paul was preaching the Word to them, they listened readily. They had an open mind. They had humble and teachable hearts. Why? Because these Bereans understood the truth about God's Word. This is an important lesson for us. If God actually speaks through the written Word, then when it is preached how can we have any other kind of posture than the posture that the Bereans had? Eagerness and a willingness to hear is one of the most practical ways in which we live out the doctrine of *Sola Scriptura*.

Eagerness and a willingness to hear is one of the most practical ways in which we live out the doctrine of Sola Scriptura.

Assuming that the preacher we are listening to is actually preaching the Word of God, we don't listen as if we are receiving a man's wisdom, which can be flawed. We don't listen with a spirit of negativity or criticism. We don't listen from a place of superiority in which we place ourselves over the Scripture and decide if we like what it says or not. We don't listen half-heartedly. We remember that it is God who is speaking through His Word, which should manifest in our eager, humble posture.

#2. We Test with the Word

There's a second application that we can draw from the Bereans. Although they received the Word through Paul with eagerness, they also *tested* his preaching by examining the Scriptures for themselves. Look again at verse 11: "They received the word with all eagerness, examining the Scriptures daily to see if these things were so." This is so important for our understanding of *Sola Scriptura* because it demonstrates that Scripture alone is the only infallible rule of truth. These Bereans were not going to rely solely on Paul's argumentation or their own experiences. They weren't going to put stock in hearsay. The Bereans knew that the Scriptures had come from the God who cannot lie. Sitting under the teaching of the great apostle himself (who had seen the risen Christ with his own eyes!), they tested what Paul said against the Scriptures. That is the vital balance that the Bereans demonstrate: both diligent study and eager humility.

If we err on one side or the other, the imbalance will show up. We don't want to become sheep who blindly receive everything we hear as if it were the Word of God.

This would be to forget that there are wolves—false teachers—who love to exploit naïve ears. On the other hand, we don't want to be negative, critical sheep who wave the flag of being "passionate about biblical accuracy" and yet have proud hearts and deaf ears that cannot receive the Word as it's being preached to us.

We need to be like the Bereans. Willing to listen. Eager. Humble. All the while holding a firm commitment that the Word of God is the only infallible authority and rule of truth.

This balanced view of the Scripture produces results. We see these results in verse 12 of Acts 17: "Many of them therefore believed." They believed! Salvation came to the Bereans that day as they examined the Scriptures, receiving the Word of God eagerly as it was taught.

#3. We Preach Expositional Sermons

As an application point for our churches, Acts 17:12 speaks powerfully to the need for expositional, exegetically sound preaching. An inerrant and authoritative Bible calls for expository preaching, in which the text is unpacked, brought to light, explained, applied. What else is there for a preacher to say apart from expounding what God has already said? Are people saved by the preacher's own ideas? By his cleverness? By his airtight outline? Will people be brought to repentance and salvation by humor, stories, or movie clips? These things may be helpful from the standpoint of communication, but they always must *serve* the Word rather than *obscure* it.

Charles Spurgeon, one of the greatest preachers to have ever lived, said this: ""If I did not believe in the infallibility of Scripture—the absolute infallibility of it from cover to cover, I would never enter this pulpit again!"[4]

Speaking of the importance of a Scripture-saturated pulpit, Steven Lawson says: "You reap what you sow, and if you sow a worldly message you will reap a worldly church. If you sow secular humanism and pop psychology and worldly trends and religious traditions and corporate leadership and cultural ideologies and philosophical thoughts and personal experiences and political commentary . . . you will reap an unconverted church. But if you sow the living and enduring Word of God you will have a regenerate church."[5]

This commitment to the public preaching of the Word isn't just for the preachers. Holding to *Sola Scriptura* also bears fruit in our daily lives. It's why we counsel people with the Word over a cup of coffee. We encourage people with the Word when we see them at the grocery store. We sing the Word in our cars on the way to work. We faithfully study the Word with brothers and sister in Christ.

It is only God's Word, by His grace and applied by His Holy Spirit to our hearts, that can bring understanding unto salvation. It's the only thing that brings real growth and transformation. It's true of us all—spiritual health in our lives is directly proportional to our intake of God's Word.

#4. We Have an External Authority

The second passage we will consider is 2 Timothy 3:14–16. The apostle Paul is writing to Timothy, a young pastor. Paul is nearing the end of his life, his long labor for Christ winding down. He's getting ready to die. The letter that he writes to Timothy is the passing of the torch to the next generation of Christian leadership.

Imagine your own life and ministry nearing its end. Imagine for a moment that you felt the burden that Paul must have felt to pass on the things most important to you—the things you *most* want those who would follow in your footsteps to remember. That is what we are reading in this passage.

Second Timothy 3:14–15 says, "But as for you, continue in what you've learned and firmly believed, knowing from whom you learned it and how from childhood you have been acquainted with the sacred writings, which are able to make you wise for salvation through faith in Christ Jesus." Paul reminds Timothy of something critical in these two verses. He reminds Timothy that the Scriptures, the sacred writings, are able to make him *wise unto salvation*. This accords perfectly with what we saw happen in the Berean church. Paul goes on to give us a description of the Word of God that is *the* bedrock verse for our understanding of *Sola Scriptura* and its practical application.

Verse 16: "All Scripture is breathed out by God." If we needed one verse—even one part of one verse—to illustrate for us how why doctrine of *Sola Scriptura* must have practical application, it is right here. All Scripture is *breathed out* by God. The Greek word is *theopneustos*, and in all of the Bible it is only used here. The very words of Scripture are the words of God Himself.

The apostle Peter echoes this idea. In 2 Peter 1:21, he says this: "Men spoke from God as they were carried along by the Holy Spirit." In other words, if you want to hear the Holy Spirit speak, you need to read

> The very words of Scripture are the words of God Himself.

your Bible! God, through His Spirit, speaks through the pages of His inspired Word. God Himself has breathed it out, and that is why we believe that Scripture is our final and sole authority. It is *theopneustos*. Here's the obvious implication: Scripture is an *external* authority. This could not be more practical for us in our day-to-day lives.

For hundreds of years, the hallmark of liberal theology that veers away from the Bible is that it rejects any external authority. If we do away with the supernatural, authoritative Word of God, then we have to place authority somewhere else. The result is that our experiences become our authority. Our feelings become our authority. Human wisdom becomes our authority. Science becomes our authority. Being on the "right side of history" becomes our authority.

But if the Scripture is God-breathed, we are not afforded the convenience of placing authority anywhere else. We are bound to the Scripture as Luther was bound. It means that we are bound to what God says about human sexuality. We are bound to what God says about marriage. We're bound to what the Word says about church structure, about how we make disciples, about how we parent our kids, about how we run our businesses. We are bound to the authority of the Word and what it says about how we can be saved. This is the day-to-day application of the doctrine of *Sola Scriptura:* we have an external authority that governs us.

If we do away with the supernatural, authoritative Word of God, then we have to place authority somewhere else.

#5. We Have A Profitable Word

Paul goes further in 2 Timothy 3:16–17. He says that the Word of God is "profitable for teaching, for reproof, for correction, for training in righteousness, that the man [or woman] of God may be complete." The Scriptures are undeniably profitable! The Holy Spirit applies their timeless truths to our hearts and our lives and we are made complete. This recalls what we previously mentioned: with the Word we speak to other people and we disciple them, or we parent them, or we offer advice to them. With the Word we reprove, and we correct errors. The Word discerns the thoughts and intentions of our own hearts and the hearts of those that we're in relationship with. By the Word we are trained in righteousness. We learn what is pleasing to God. We memorize it. We meditate on it. By the Word we are equipped for every good work. In other words, your Christian ministry is fueled by the truth of the Scripture. Psalm 119:105 says, "Your word is a lamp unto my feet and a light to my path."

As in all things, Jesus is the greatest example of reverence for the Word of God. Jesus Himself demonstrated a commitment to the perfection and centrality of the Word of God. Over and over Jesus placed His trust in the written Scriptures. Whether it was preaching in the temple, praying the Psalms, walking the long road toward Golgotha, or teaching from the Scriptures after His resurrection, Jesus was saturated with the Word of God. You might say that Jesus loved His Bible!

As one specific and practical example, think of Jesus in the wilderness of temptation. Forty days and forty nights Satan assaulted Him with temptation. How did Jesus fight the Devil? By quoting the Scriptures. In Matthew 4, Jesus said three separate times "it is written." Christian, if you want hope and victory in light of your own temptations, then open your Bible and say, "It is written!"

Jesus Himself demonstrated a commitment to the perfection and centrality of the Word of God.

"It is written, 'Man shall not live by bread alone but by every word that comes from the mouth of God'" (Matthew 4:4). The Word of God brings freedom and life to the person who is willing to eat it like bread!

There's no better strategy for growth in your life than a steady diet of His Word. Do you believe that to be true? Or do you rely on human wisdom, self-help, or positive thinking? Is your faith in God really just a flimsy spirituality—a hodgepodge of the ideas that you like best? Is your spiritual growth overly dependent on your emotional experiences? Do your religious traditions matter to you more than what God has said in His Word? Is your authority vested in the whims of our culture?

Paul's final charge to Timothy in light of this all-sufficient, inerrant, and authoritative Word of God is found in 2 Timothy 4:1–2. Listen to the power in the words that he writes to Timothy: "I charge you in the presence of God and of Christ Jesus, who is to judge the living and the dead, and by his appearing, and his kingdom, preach the word." Preach the Word! Of all the things that the apostle Paul could have left with Timothy, anything he could have reiterated as his life neared its end, he charges this young man to preach the Word. May we remember the infinite value and the explosive power of the eternal and abiding Word of God.

As a closing thought, let us consider our own sinfulness. Because of our sinfulness, do you realize that God owes us nothing but silence? In our sin, we deserved punishment. We deserved to be cut off from His voice. Because all of us have fallen short of God's glory and turned to our own way, silence would've been a perfectly just response.

And yet—in love, God speaks! He is the one that pursued Adam and Eve in the garden. They were running from Him and He said, "Where are you?" He spoke to them. He came and found them. This is a God who is loving and gracious and kind, and delights to reveal Himself to sinful people. Through His Word, He draws us to Himself that we might trust in Christ, that we might be forgiven, that we might be saved and sanctified for all of eternity. He speaks through His Word that we might be one day glorified in His very presence. The gospel of Christ in the Bible is nothing short of the love of God recorded for us.

That is why we love the Word—because it leads us to a knowledge of this eternally gracious God. The Scriptures that we hold in our hands are a gift of unsurpassed worth. May they be our sole, unshakeable foundation!

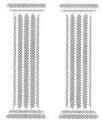

SOLUS CHRISTUS

(Christ Alone)

There are few things more awe-inspiring or more humbling than beholding Jesus as the only way to salvation and understanding what that means. *Solus Christus.* Christ alone. So much more than merely a doctrinal truth, the reality of salvation in Christ alone should set our hearts on fire for the glory of God!

Overarching the Reformers' drive to answer the question of how sinful people can be made right with a holy God, there was a rift between Protestant theology and the Catholic Church. The Catholic Church's teaching was (and is) that salvation was found in Jesus Christ AND . . . Jesus AND good works. Jesus AND baptism. Jesus AND mass AND confession AND prayers to the saints AND, AND, AND . . . As you can imagine, no one ever knew if they were okay with God. "Jesus AND" theology plagued them with questions. Have I done enough? Am I doing enough now? The truth is that many people live the same way today. This could even be you.

The Reformers, on the other hand, said, "No! That's not how salvation works." Martin Luther, John Calvin, Ulrich Zwingli, John Knox, John Wycliffe, William Tyndale, and a host of other Reformers staunchly omitted the "ANDs" so prevalent in the Catholic Church.

So much more than merely a doctrinal truth, the reality of salvation in Christ alone should set our hearts on fire for the glory of God!

What they were left with was *Christ alone.*

The Latin word for *and* is *et*. It has been said that you can boil down the Reformation to the difference between two words: *et* or *sola*. Christ *and*, or Christ *alone*.

What Does *Solus Christus* Mean?

It's important to understand what exactly the Reformers meant when they said "Christ alone." The Reformers were not necessarily emphasizing that Christ is the only way to salvation, although He *is*! Jesus is the way, the truth, and the life. There aren't other options. There's *one* option, and it's Jesus Christ. Along with the Reformers and the Bible itself, the Catholic Church at the time of the Reformation would have believed in Christ's exclusivity—the exclusive nature of Christ alone as the source of our salvation. They would have affirmed with the Reformers verses such as these, which we cherish when we think of Christ as the way to salvation:

- John 14:6 —"Jesus said to him, 'I am the way, and the truth, and the life. No one comes to the Father except through me.'"

- Acts 4:12 —"And there is salvation in no one else, for there is no other name under heaven given among men by which we must be saved."

- 1 Timothy 2:5 —"For there is one God, and there is one mediator between God and men, the man Christ Jesus."

- Romans 10:9 —"If you confess with your mouth that Jesus is Lord and you believe in your heart that God raised him from the dead, you will be saved."

- John 3:18 —"Whoever believes in him is not condemned, but whoever does not believe is condemned already, because he has not believed in the name of the only Son of God."

However, the Reformers were in disagreement with the Catholic Church regarding the *sufficiency* of Christ's death and resurrection for our salvation. In other words, when the Reformers spoke of Christ alone, here's what they were saying: Christ alone is *enough* for our salvation. The cross is *enough*. The work of Jesus through His death and resurrection is *enough*—perfectly sufficient for the salvation of sinners likes us.

This is precisely what *Solus Christus* means. It means that salvation is not found in "Jesus AND" or "Jesus PLUS" anything. Rather, salvation is found through the sufficient work of Christ's life, death, and resurrection alone. It's a sufficiency issue. The Bible is crystal clear on this. We do not need anything added to Jesus' finished work on the cross to be saved. We are saved by Christ alone. That gives us reason to rejoice! That's why we sing! Because it is in Christ alone that our hope is found and that we are saved.

We do not need anything added to Jesus' finished work on the cross to be saved. We are saved by Christ alone.

The Personal Testimony of Paul

Let's consider Philippians 3:1–8 and some of the ways this verse reveals the glory of *Solus Christus*. This is a passage in which the apostle Paul is making it evident that we are not saved by anything other than the person and the work of Jesus Christ. "Finally, my brothers, rejoice in the Lord. To write the same things to you is no trouble to me and is safe for you" (v. 1). Paul is reminding these brothers and sisters in Philippi of the core truths of their faith in order to protect them spiritually (and by extension to protect us as well).

"Look out for the dogs, look out for the evil doers, look out for those who mutilate the flesh" (v. 2). To whom is Paul referring? He's specifically talking about a group of individuals who are called the Judaizers. They were "Jesus AND" guys. They were passionate individuals who would pursue new Christians. Paul has caught wind of them, and he's warning the Philippian church.

Note that every cult in the history of the world starts this same way. Cults today prey especially on those who are young in the faith. They also prey on those who have been poorly instructed in the Bible. These individuals may have been fired up for Jesus, but there's no rootedness; there's no doctrinal foundation. Cults grow by going after these types of people. Paul knows this, so he exhorts the Philippians to be on their guard!

Paul continues in verse 3, "For we are the circumcision, who worship by the Spirit of God and glory in Christ Jesus and put no confidence in the flesh." The true circumcision, Paul says, are those who are true Christians—those who have been regenerated, born again by the Holy Spirit, and who have genuine faith in Christ and Christ alone as Lord and Savior. Paul is emphasizing that our salvation is not based on "Jesus AND" or "Jesus PLUS . . .

" In particular, he is saying it's not contingent on any feature, like physical, *external* circumcision, which the Judaizers believed. Rather, salvation is based on *true* circumcision. This New Testament language is a language of the heart. It's a new heart that God gives us by His grace in Christ—and by the power of the Spirit, we've been given this new heart at the moment of our true conversion to Christ.

This new heart is marked by a few things according to verse 3: the true worship of God, living for the glory of Jesus, and putting *no* confidence in the flesh. In other words, we aren't that big of a deal. God is. We can't impress Him or pay our own way, because Christ has already impressed and paid on our behalf!

Next, Paul takes us to what is really the heart of this passage. In verses 4–6, he gives a testimony about his own life. Not only that, he shows us how we are saved by Christ's work alone and not by an outstanding résumé or good deeds, as if we could impress God or somehow earn His approval. Paul lists seven ways that, before he became a Christian, he believed would earn his salvation. These are the "Jesus ANDs" of Paul's unconverted life. Looking back on his life, the apostle Paul lists these things and counts them as spiritual loss—not gain. In the eyes of world, these seven things had brought him great gain. Paul had reckoned the same must be true in the eyes of God, but after meeting Christ on the road to Damascus he realizes he had been completely wrong.

Starting in Philippians 3:4, Paul says, " . . . though I myself have reason for confidence in the flesh also." He's saying, "I've done a lot of stuff that's pretty impressive." Then he continues in verse 4, "If anyone else thinks he has reason for confidence in the flesh, I have more." He is going even further by saying, "If you're going to try to persuade me that somehow you can earn your way to heaven or you can earn God's approval of you . . . then I'm the most impressive guy around." And using a human scale of achievement, he was! Paul is laboring in these few verses to demolish the argument that we can do anything to save ourselves.

Let's briefly examine these seven things and see what Paul is saying. How do they apply to us, and how do they reiterate the doctrine of salvation in Christ alone?

#1. Salvation Is Not Found in Ritual

Paul says in verse 5, "circumcised on the eighth day." He starts at the very beginning of his life. The point that he is underlining is the purity of his Jewish background. He was born into a family that kept the regulations of Old Testament circumcision precisely; it was the most essential ritual and rite in Judaism. Paul is really stepping on religious toes here, but he wants us to know that we aren't saved by a ritual like circumcision, or any other ritual for that matter!

How often can we find comfort in adherence to our church attendance, taking the Lord's Supper, or listening to a sermon. In their proper place in our hearts, these things should help us mature. But they don't save us. All the trappings of religious ritual contribute nothing to salvation.

All the trappings of religious ritual contribute nothing to salvation.

#2. Salvation Is Not Found in One's Race

Paul continues in verse 5, " . . . of the people of Israel." Paul was a true Jew; he was born into God's people. He was a part of the nation chosen by God from the very beginning. Paul wasn't one of those "Gentile converts." He was the real deal. Here's what he is saying: in the same way that we're not saved by circumcision or religious ritual, we're not saved by our racial heritage. Our pedigree counts for nothing when it comes to salvation.

This is a pervasive problem in our world today as we see people divided by racial tension. In our sin, we can wrestle with an innate sense that our racial heritage is superior, somehow earning more of God's special attention. And while God did have a special plan for Israel, it was through Israel that *all* nations would be blessed by the coming of Christ. Our race contributes nothing to salvation.

#3. Salvation Is Not Found in One's Social Circles

Again, in verse 5, Paul gives his next point of former confidence: " . . . of the tribe of Benjamin." Not only was Paul a true Jew, but he was a part of the best, most respected tribe . . . the Benjamites! That may not impress us, but it impressed the Jews. But Paul's privileged status as a Benjamite did not impress God. Family or social status doesn't save you.

The reality is that some of us are banking on Grandma's faith to get us into heaven. Have you ever heard the generalized sentiment, "He or she prayed a lot for me, so I'm hoping I'm in"? People may have had godly parents or kids or even grandkids on whose coattails they're trying to ride. But that's not how it works. We're not saved through the faith of someone else, or by being a part of an elite religious club. We're saved when we place our faith, by God's grace, in Christ alone.

> *The reality is that some of us are banking on Grandma's faith to get us into heaven.*

#4. Salvation Is Not Found in Education

Paul goes on in verse 5, saying he was "a Hebrew of Hebrews." Why is that significant? Well, Paul not only spoke Hebrew, but he studied Hebrew under the greatest scholar of the day, a man named Gamaliel. Whoever studied under Gamaliel had arrived. The individual who studied under Gamaliel was a top scholar; he knew everything and could out-argue anyone. He had a Harvard-level education; he had the best training in the law that a man could have. This was Paul's educational heritage. Of course, there is nothing wrong with having an impressive education. We want to know theology, we want to know the Word, we want to grow. We want to love God with all of our mind. But, sadly, there are a lot of people who know a lot *about* Jesus but don't love Jesus. Satan himself has really "good" theology. But airtight theology doesn't save anyone.

These first four traits were Paul's pedigree; these were inherited or afforded to him by nature of his birth into the nation of Israel. Now we're going to see a shift: the final three reasons for former confidence that Paul lists are things that he pursued in his own effort to put himself over

We want to love God with all of our mind. But, sadly, there are a lot of people who know a lot about Jesus but don't love Jesus.

the top. If you think the first four items on his résumé are impressive, he goes even further.

#5. Salvation Is Not Found in Religious Code

Verse 5 again: "as to the law," Paul says, "a Pharisee." Remember, the Pharisees were a Jewish sect. Literally, the name means "separated ones." The Pharisees were deeply committed to the strict obedience of the law of God. They were seen as the spiritual A-listers. In order to obey the law of God, they put into place a massive list of additional requirements that had to be followed in order to *really* please the Lord.

In essence, the Pharisees were saying, "If you're really committed, then you're going to follow all these other laws too." And in this verse Paul is saying, "I was that guy. In fact, I was the leader of those guys." And he was. He was a Pharisee of Pharisees. But by the grace of God, Paul realized that a person can be incredibly religious and remain unconverted. Salvation is not gained because of some radical commitment to religion in hopes of pleasing God.

#6. Salvation Is Not Found in One's Passion

Paul continues in verse 6: "as to zeal, a persecutor of the church." Here's what Paul is saying: "You want to find someone who was zealous? I was zealous. I was so zealous that I persecuted believers. I oversaw the death of Christians." Paul fervently believed that was what God wanted. He believed his unquenchable passion would earn him points with God.

Of course, zeal and passion for God are really good things. In fact, we need far *more* passion and zeal for Christ in the church—not less! We need *more* sold-out followers of Jesus who unapologetically love Him and His Word!

But verse 6 reminds us that passion and zeal, when disconnected from saving faith, can go south very quickly. The Bible speaks of this in certain places as "zeal without knowledge." In Romans 10:1, Paul writes, "Brothers, my heart's desire and prayer to God for them is that they may be saved." He's speaking particularly of the very religious, very zealous Pharisees. But in verse 2, notice what he says: "For I bear them witness that they have zeal for God, but not according to knowledge."

We need to spend a bit more time on this particular point, given the trends of our culture. If you're paying attention, it won't take long to observe that passion and truth are often equated in our world today. The measure of zeal that a person has for a particular belief is often confused for the truthfulness of the belief itself.

Another way of saying "zeal without knowledge" is "ignorance on fire." People can say they're passionate about God but don't truly know the God they claim to worship. It's a shallow emotionalism. It's not rooted in doctrinal truth. Paul had zeal. He was passionate . . . but not about the truth. Before his conversion, he couldn't even see the truth!

The same can be true for us today, and that reality demands our humility. We can be very passionate and zealous about any number of things—even things that we think God is zealous about—and be completely wrong. We can be passionate about things that aren't even in line with who God is or what He's revealed in His Word. We need to be on guard. We are so drawn to passion, in and of itself, that we can be duped pretty easily.

This is true not only of individuals in our culture, but of many churches as well. Churches can be very passionate about particular things—but are they passionate about the truth of the gospel and the Word of God? That's the question. This is why a historical, biblical, orthodox faith is so critical for the mission of the church. Rootedness in the Scriptures can help us discern right from wrong, good from bad. We can ask each other (and ask of churches), "Is this a good thing to be zealous about, or is it not?" Otherwise, we fall into ignorance on fire.

> *Churches can be very passionate about particular things—but are they passionate about the truth of the gospel and the Word of God?*

Where we live, in Denver, people are lost and longing for Jesus. They just don't know it. The same is true in your city. These people do not need churches and Christians who are marked by ignorance on fire. They don't need a short emotional high. They need the truth of the gospel that will transform their very being. That's what we must be about.

Paul's point in Philippians 3:6 is this: you may be genuinely sincere and passionate for the things of God. But your zeal and your passion do not save you.

#7. Salvation Is Not Found in Rule-Keeping

In the last part of verse 6, Paul writes, "as to righteousness under the law, blameless." If there ever were a great rule-follower, it would be Paul. And he knew it. Everybody knew it. He could speak with integrity. He loved rules, and he was the shining example of following them.

Everything was right about Paul . . . on the outside. And that's the critical issue. Some of us are really good at following rules. But what about our hearts? External rule-following and a heart far from God are a dangerous combination. The underlying narrative of that kind of life sounds like this: "I'm a good rule-follower, but I'm not very authentic with people. I can easily give the impression of being somebody that I'm not because I don't want others to

> *External rule-following and a heart far from God are a dangerous combination.*

see for a second that I might be broken. That I might not be perfect. That I might need Jesus—*for real.*" When you bring these two things together—rule-following with a heart that doesn't belong to the Lord—you are left with a dead religion. And, of course, dead religion does not save anybody.

In light of all seven things Paul has shared about his life, here is what he is trying to communicate: The only way to be saved is Christ alone. He culminates his line of thought in verse 7, "But whatever gain I had, I counted as loss for the sake of Christ." The word loss can be interpreted as "worthless." You can literally translate it dung. It stinks. It's putrid. It's gross.

God had done something profound and irreversible in Paul's life: by His grace and His grace alone, God opened Paul's eyes to see that everything he thought was righteous and good—the things on which he was counting—was actually keeping him from being right before God. Jesus didn't have Paul's heart, and that was the watershed issue.

There is a challenge for us in this list from Paul's life. We need to ask ourselves if there are ways in which we view our own lives as Paul had viewed his. In other words, are there things in your life—in your family, in your morality, in your religious accomplishments—that you've been trusting in? Are there any "Jesus ANDs" in your life? There are subtle ways in which we can fall into this very mind-set, content to do the right things and fool everybody until the very end. The Bible's clear message helps us to identify those things and to recognize that they do not save us. Only Christ saves.

Our hearts must be humble and tender, recognizing our frailty and Christ's sufficiency. Everything must flow out of a life that is genuine, in which we're becoming less and Jesus is becoming more. Otherwise, all we are doing is living like a good Pharisee.

Do you see how radical this is? This is how different Christianity is from every other religion. All other religions are based on works. They are based on what you do or what you don't do. And the thinking is that if you do enough good and not too much bad, ultimately, you'll please God somehow. He'll let you into heaven, won't He? But the gospel of Christianity is the opposite. It says that you aren't ever going to be good enough. And you don't have to be, because Christ was good *in your place.* He alone paid the debt of our failures so that we can be saved though faith in Him. This is the good news of the gospel.

People say this seems too good to be true. It does seem too good to be true, but it *is* true, and that's the heart of our God. Take the time to ask God to reveal your heart. If you're trying to be a good person on your own, you're never going to live a truly joyful life in God. You have to recognize Christ is all.

Solus Christus leads us to live lives of joyful submission and obedience. We don't do a bunch of good deeds in order to be approved of by God; we do them because of what's been done for us in Christ. When Christ takes over our lives and the Spirit infuses us, we begin to live with a different goal in mind—the glory of God and not self.

> *When Christ takes over our lives and the Spirit infuses us, we begin to live with a different goal in mind—the glory of God and not self.*

It's the natural outflow of a redeemed life. Christ—not my ego—becomes my treasure. That's what a heartfelt devotion to the doctrine of *Solus Christus* does in us.

Paul concludes that in light of all his accomplishments and all the reasons he should have been approved by God, it was all worthless apart from Christ. He goes on in verse 8, "Indeed, I count everything as loss because of the surpassing worth of knowing Christ Jesus my Lord."

Why does Paul say this? The whole point of Philippians 3:1–8 is this: *Salvation is not found in our work for Christ. It is found in Christ's work for us.* By His grace and mercy alone! We rejoice because this message is true! How can we not then sing and praise and live for His glory?

The Practical Realities of *Solus Christus*

Solus Christus is not just some doctrine by which we stand amazed. It's a principle that should change our lives every day. How is this good news for us? How do we apply this truth to our everyday lives as Christians?

I want to outline eight reasons why Solus Christus is good news. And "good news" doesn't even capture it. It's unbelievable news! It's the kind of news that causes us to live radical lives of faith for the sake of Christ and His glory.

#1. Only in Christ Alone Am I a New Creation

> 2 Corinthians 5:17 —"Therefore, if anyone is in Christ, he is a new creation. The old has passed away; behold, the new has come."

Christ makes you new. You don't make yourself new. A new self-help strategy isn't going to help you become new. The only one who can make you new is the living God through Christ, making you a new creation. This isn't something that the Reformers invented or the modern church has stumbled upon. This is what Scripture teaches us clearly. Only in Christ alone are you a new creation.

#2. Only in Christ Alone Am I Chosen by God

> Ephesians 1:3–4 —" Blessed be the God and Father of our Lord Jesus Christ, who has blessed us in Christ with every spiritual blessing in the heavenly places, even as he chose us in him before the foundation of the world, that we should be holy and blameless before him."

God chose you in Christ, before the foundation of the world, to be holy and blameless in His sight! If there was ever a doubt of God's gracious love for you, consider that you have been chosen in Christ before the world existed.

#3. Only in Christ Alone Am I Adopted as His Child

> John 1:12 —"But to all who did receive him, who believed in his name, he gave the right to become children of God . . ."

Some of us have been looking for a family to belong to our whole lives. And you know what Jesus is saying to you today? "Come to Me and be part of the family of God. Be accepted. Be adored. Be a child of God." Jesus died that we might be adopted as sons and daughters of the King.

Much has been written before about this, but I want to briefly point out that one of our fundamental issues as human beings is that we live in this constant state of identity crisis. We're trying to find our identity in all kinds of things. As Christians, it's something we struggle with. For non-Christians, it's a constant state of being. People find their identities in a wide range of things. This includes titles like "soccer mom" or "life of the party." Or it involves your job or living in a good neighborhood or wearing certain clothes or listening to particular music. Your identity is intricately linked with all of those things that make you feel safe, loved, important, or unique. We try to find our identity in anything and everything, and we're totally confused. In our sin, that's what happens. We are idolaters, and we're looking for all manner of things to satisfy us and to give us identity.

You know how to end your identity crisis? You bow the knee at the cross of Christ. And you place your faith in Him and be adopted as a son or daughter of the King. That's your identity now. Is there anything greater? Our identity is not in some "value title" the world gives you or that you strive for in vain. The Christian is a son or daughter of God! Loved by Him! Died for! Reconciled to God! That's your identity, and I say in love for you: quit trying to find your identity in something else. It will never satisfy. Because you were made to be identified with Christ and in Christ alone.

You know how to end your identity crisis? You bow the knee at the cross of Christ.

#4. Only in Christ Alone Am I Redeemed and Forgiven of All My Sins

> Colossians 1:13–14 —"He has delivered us from the domain of darkness and transferred us to the kingdom of his beloved Son, in whom we have redemption, the forgiveness of sins."

Let's be crystal clear. You are not forgiven by any other means than the sufficient work of Jesus Christ. Consider your past. All of those things that embarrass you, all of those things that you hope nobody ever discovers about you. Jesus died to cover them all. His blood covers our past, present, and future. We are forgiven through Christ and Christ alone. We are redeemed! Do you know what redemption entails? Restoring broken things. That is what God is about. Restoring broken people like you and me. We are broken, but God is glorified in His acts of redemption. He is glorified in extending and showing forgiveness to sinners like us.

It is only in Christ alone that we find this kind of forgiveness and redemption. Again, if you are someone who lives in constant guilt, shame, and fear of your past: Jesus Christ says, "Bring it all to Me. Let Me take it all. I died for *all*. You don't need to carry any of it. And then when you pick it back up again, bring it back to Me. I'm not going to be mad because you brought it back. Just bring it back to Me, over and over and over again. Because I've paid it all. I want you to live in a new freedom and in a new life and a new joy." That's our Lord and King.

#5. Only in Christ Alone Am I Justified before a Holy God

> Romans 5:1 —"Therefore, since we have been justified by faith, we have peace with God through our Lord Jesus Christ."

Sola Fide, which we'll cover in chapter 4 , means "Faith Alone." We see in this verse that the two doctrines of *Sola Fide* and *Solus Christus* are inseparable. Because of Christ, we are at peace with God now. This is the God against whom we have rebelled—the God who is righteous and holy and whose wrath against our sin is completely justified. But Christ Jesus on the cross bears the wrath of God that we had earned. He takes it upon Himself, so that through faith in Him, we don't have to experience the wrath of God for our sin. That's justification. Only in Christ alone am I justified before a holy God.

#6. Only in Christ Alone Am I Complete

> Colossians 2:9–10 —"For in him the whole fullness of deity dwells bodily and you have been filled in him, who is the head of all rule and authority."

Fullness! What a beautiful word in this text! Take a moment to let this sink in: You are full in Christ. And, by the way, He is King over everything. That's who makes you full. While contemplating the meaning of fullness in our culture, I thought of the movie *Jerry Maguire*. There is a scene in which Tom Cruise says to Renee Zellweger, "You complete me." But here's the truth: No person can complete you! This is a lie in our culture. Young lovers in our world today must be reminded that no lover can satisfy them. This lie causes a host of problems because we have an expectation that "he/she should complete me." But another person can't complete you . . . and, by the way, you can't complete another person either. Christ alone completes us! This truth frees us to love and be loved without false expectations.

That verse is about far more than being completely loved. We are also regenerated, empowered, gifted, convicted, given daily grace and a million other things by His Spirit!

#7. Only in Christ Alone Am I Declared the Righteousness of God

> 2 Corinthians 5:21 —"For our sake he made him to be sin who knew no sin, so that in him we might become the righteousness of God."

On the cross, Jesus quite literally became sin. He knew no sin; He was the perfect sacrifice. On the cross, Christ took the wrath of God on our behalf. Through faith in Jesus, we are given His perfect righteousness. In spite of our sin, when God sees us, we are covered in the perfect righteousness of Christ. Which is why the Father can say, "Come home to Me." Because apart from the righteousness of Christ, we're in serious trouble. We could never be right before a holy God on our own because we are in deep sin and rebellion against Him from the beginning.

The only reason we can be accepted and enter into the very presence of God both now and for eternity is because of the work of Christ on our behalf. He is the only one who *makes* us righteous, so that God can *declare* us righteous!

#8. Only in Christ Alone Am I Free from Condemnation—I Cannot Be Separated from God's Love

I want to point back to the great Reformer Martin Luther with the question we've considered in this book: how can sinful men and women be made right with a holy God? This is the question that would literally keep Luther up night after night. This was his biggest fear. Before his conversion, he would be haunted by the thought, *I know I'm sinful. I'm afraid of this God and what He's going to do to me. I'm afraid to die.* This is what drove Luther until he found in the Scriptures the good news of this chapter: *Solus Christus.* We are saved *in Christ alone.*

In closing, I want to bring this to our attention and stand amazed at the love of God for us through Christ. The apostle Paul writes in Romans 8:31–39:

> What then shall we say to these things? If God is for us, who can be against us? He who did not spare his own Son but gave him up for us all, how will he not also with him graciously give us all things? Who shall bring any charge against God's elect? It is God who justifies. Who is to condemn? Christ Jesus is the one who died—more than that, who was raised—who is at the right hand of God, who indeed is interceding for us. Who shall separate us from the love of Christ? Shall tribulation, or distress, or persecution, or famine, or nakedness, or danger, or sword? As it is written,
>
> > "For your sake we are being killed all the day long;
> > we are regarded as sheep to be slaughtered."
>
> No, in all these things we are more than conquerors through him who loved us. For I am sure that neither death nor life, nor angels nor rulers, nor things present nor things to come, nor powers, nor height nor depth, nor anything else in all creation, will be able to separate us from the love of God in Christ Jesus our Lord.

The good news of Solus Christus—of the gospel itself—is that we are saved NOT by "Jesus AND" anything.

The good news of Solus Christus—of the gospel itself—is that we are saved NOT by "Jesus AND" anything. Rather, when we humble ourselves, repent of our sins, and place our faith and our trust in Christ alone, we are saved by Christ ALONE!

SOLA GRATIA

(Grace Alone)

Grace is at the very center of our salvation. We often repeat the phrase, in song or prayer, that we are *saved by grace*. Rightly so! The grace of God is the subject of the most famous hymn ever written. Grace is the subject matter of stirring sermons and rousing choruses. But at times, the ever-present force of grace in our lives can be taken for granted. We don't really think about it much beyond it being a catchphrase. And yet, apart from grace, the very fabric of what we believe about our salvation would unravel. But before we can be reminded again of the power of grace, we need to remember the bad news.

The Need for Grace

Our culture today seems inordinately obsessed with zombies—books, TV shows, movies—we find fascinating the idea of animated corpses. Dead men walking have a way of capturing our collective imagination.

In Ephesians 2, the apostle Paul describes a human condition that sounds a lot like what we have come to call a zombie. Understanding Paul's reasoning in this passage is critical if we are to properly understand the beauty of grace. To

We don't really think about it much beyond it being a catchphrase. And yet, apart from grace, the very fabric of what we believe about our salvation would unravel.

appreciate the good news, we have to come face-to-face with the bad news. The seriousness of who we were before we were Christians. We have to understand our position *before* grace entered in.

Ephesians 2:1–2 says, "And you were dead in the trespasses and sins in which you once walked, following the course of this world, following the prince of the power of the air, the spirit that is now at work in the sons of disobedience." In this verse, Paul is describing for the Ephesian Christians their condition before they were saved by Christ. He is describing a zombie. The Ephesians were getting up in the morning, they were going to the market, they were doing their work, they were preparing their dinner, they were going back to bed . . . but they weren't really alive. They were following—walking—in the path that their flesh and that the world had set before them.

They had a leader that they were following as well: the prince of the power of the air. In other words, Satan himself was their leader. In their sin against God, because they had broken His laws, because they did not love Him, the Ephesians were spiritual corpses.

If the Ephesians' awful condition before Christ sounds bad, the next verse gets even worse. Paul continues in verse 3: "among whom we all once lived in the passions of our flesh, carrying out the desires of the body and the mind."

In those three short verses we have to come to grips with a crushing truth. All of us share a common and insurmountable problem, and that problem is that *all* of us were spiritually dead. And our spiritual death led us into indulge our sinfulness. Paul says that we were living in the passions of our flesh, carrying out the desires of the body and of the mind. If we could think of something sick or depraved—we would do it. If a harsh word sprang to our minds—we would speak it. If we wanted sexual gratification—we would go find it. If by lying we could gain—then lie we would. Whatever fleshly and debased thing the world offered us, we would snatch it. That is not to say we were as evil as we could possibly be, for even non-Christians can do good things. But it is to say that we *all* were once spiritually dead.

It's important for us to understand the depth of this depravity. We were not just spiritually sick; we were not getting better with some self-effort; we were not intrinsically good people that society had corrupted. Sometimes we may be tempted to think that people's biggest problem is the spiritual equivalent of the common cold. We'd like to think we are going to be alright; we're not that bad off; we're going to pull through.

But that isn't how the Bible talks about our pre-conversion condition! The Word of God loudly proclaims to us that we were dead. And if there is one thing that is true of dead people, it is that dead people don't get better. We were depraved to the uttermost, unable to pull ourselves out of our own spiritual graves.

The bad news continues to mount in Ephesians 2 as Paul tells us that our spiritual death, our trespass, and our sin *earned* us something. Verse 3 says: "we were by nature children of wrath, like the rest of mankind." In other words, spiritually dead people have a destiny: to face the wrath of a holy God against our

The Word of God loudly proclaims to us that we were dead. And if there is one thing that is true of dead people, it is that dead people don't get better.

rebellion. The point that Paul is making is crystal clear—all of us, before Christ, were awaiting the swift and just punishment of God Himself. We had no hope of escape. No one person was in any better position before God than the next.

In Romans 3:22–23 Paul levels the playing field for every human being who has ever lived: "For there is no distinction, for all have sinned and fall short of the glory of God." Do we feel the weight of that? The hopelessness of it all?

What is it that we need? The answer, of course, is the third of the *Solas*: *Sola Gratia*.

The Source of Grace

Ephesians 2:4 begins with what may be the two sweetest words in the whole of the Scriptures. The great Welsh preacher D. Martyn Lloyd-Jones said, "These two words, in and of themselves, in a sense contain the whole of the gospel." Precious beyond comprehension, these two words are "*but God*." Ephesians 2:4–5 reads,

> . . . but God, being rich in mercy, because of the great love with which he loved us, even when we were dead in our trespasses made us alive together, with Christ, by grace you have been saved.

Verse 4 could have read "and God." And God gave you what you deserved. And God justly punished every sinner. Praise the Lord, that is not what we read! We read BUT GOD—in extravagant mercy He spares us from His wrath. But God loved us with a great love. But God made us alive with Christ, by grace we have been saved. The source of grace is ever and only God. It did not originate with us!

To understand the doctrine of *Sola Gratia* is to understand that grace it is not earned, it is not merited, it is not deserved. We couldn't cooperate with His grace. We couldn't add to it. We couldn't supplement it or improve upon it. We couldn't find it or win it or buy it. It was simply given to us. Pure, sovereign grace.

In Romans 3:21–24 we see this gift of grace on full display: "But now the righteousness of God has been manifested apart from the law, although the Law and the Prophets bear witness to it—the righteousness of God through faith in Jesus Christ for all that believe. For there is no distinction: for all have sinned and fall short of the glory of God, and are justified by his grace as a gift, through the redemption that is in Christ Jesus."

The gift of grace is the turning point in the story of salvation. But it is not an inactive gift. The gift of grace is not like the kind of gift that you receive that then collects dust in your closet. The gift of grace is not something that you receive only to give it away at the next white elephant party. Rather, this gift of grace *accomplishes* something in the life of the believer. Sinners are *justified*, or declared righteous, by His grace. All have sinned, but it is God's

> *The gift of grace is the turning point in the story of salvation. But it is not an inactive gift.*

undeserved kindness that in grace He gives spiritual life and righteousness to spiritually dead people who contributed nothing.

Romans 5:6 says, "For while we were still weak, at the right time, Christ died for the ungodly." Christ died for ungodly people, not people who had contributed. First John 4:10 says, "In this is love, not that we've loved God, but that he loved us and sent his Son to be the propitiation for our sins." Christ took God's wrath on our behalf, not because we loved God, but because God loved us. Grace stands alone.

At this point we might ask, *"Why does God in grace save sinners?"* If we truly understand our spiritual depravity, then our answer to that question can never be *"because God saw in me something worthwhile. God saved me because I brought something to the table. God saved me because I was endearing or better than the next person."* No, the answer to the question is that God saves sinners because it pleases Him to do it. We are the recipients of an extravagant goodness. And that was the great Protestant insight of salvation during the Reformation: salvation is *always* initiated by God. *Sola Gratia.* It is grace alone that brings us to Christ, and as we saw in the previous chapter, it is Christ alone who saves.

And that was the great Protestant insight of salvation during the Reformation: salvation is always initiated by God.

The Practical Realities of *Sola Gratia*

Let's jump back to Ephesians. In chapter 2, Paul has shown us the clear need that we have for grace. And we have seen that the source of that grace is God Himself. But Paul goes on in the next few verses of Ephesians 2 to describe the results of grace: "Even when we were dead in our trespasses, [he] made us alive together with Christ—by grace you have been saved—and raised us up with him and seated us with him in the heavenly places in Christ Jesus" (vv. 5–6).

#1. Abundant Life

The first result of grace is abundant life! In Christ we have been made alive, and it is not just a theoretical kind of life. If being made alive in Christ becomes no more than an abstract theological idea, then the world will become more and more attractive to us. The things that we can experience, taste, touch, and see in this world will seduce us if we forget this reality of abundant life in Christ. Any kind of life apart from life in Christ is a farce. It's a weak substitute for being raised up with the Lord Jesus and seated with Him in the heavenly places. A life that is lived

> *If being made alive in Christ becomes no more than an abstract theological idea, then the world will become more and more attractive to us.*

pursuing the trinkets of this world is a counterfeit kind of life.

But the Christian has been saved by grace and been given life in abundance. If you're a Christian, you used to be dead but now you are alive! We were all, once, like Lazarus. Dead and buried but given life by Jesus. Can you imagine anything else that would have defined Lazarus's life after Jesus raised him from the dead? Imagine how silly it would be for Lazarus to center his second life around his money, job, or earthly relationships. How could worldly pleasures ever eclipse the miracle of walking out of a tomb? What was true of Lazarus is true of us.

#2. Assurance of Salvation

The next result of grace comes in verse 7 of Ephesians 2: "so that in the coming ages he might show the immeasurable riches of his grace in kindness toward us in Christ Jesus." *Sola Gratia* gives us assurance of our salvation. Verse 7 is future tense. We've been raised up and saved by grace alone *so that* in the future God can keep showing you the immeasurable riches of His grace. It goes on and on and on. That is the reason we will be with Him forever. It's an eternity in which we celebrate God's kindness to us. But that kind of eternity is not a guarantee if we can somehow lose our salvation. How could Paul have written that verse if people who were spiritually dead could be made spiritually alive—only to become spiritually dead again when grace ran dry?

Some people see God as an angry parent, maybe someday getting mad enough that He would kick us out of the house. We look at the sin that we have committed and we are so overcome, so crippled by guilt and by shame, that we can't possibly imagine an eternity in the presence of the Lord. But the Bible has a different message. The Bible says if it is by grace alone that you have been saved, then it is by grace you will be preserved. Preserved so that God can continually show us His grace forever.

The Bible says if it is by grace alone that you have been saved, then it is by grace you will be preserved.

#3. Humility

The next result is humility. Ephesians 2:8–9 says: "For by grace you have been saved through faith. And this is not your own doing; it is the gift of God, not a result of works, so that no one may boast." Grace produces humility. If you are proud, if you are arrogant, if you look down on others who don't love God as much as you love God, if you think more highly of yourself because you know so much or because you do so much or because you're the only one that "gets" the gospel, then you have not understood *Sola Gratia.*

God did not save you because you smelled better than the corpse next to you.

Oftentimes we can be guilty of prideful, arrogant attitudes. Sometimes it's external, but more often it is internal. Our pride can be easy to spot or it can be buried under false humility. But our flesh is hard-wired for boasting in how great we are. Grace teaches us another way. Grace reminds us that our salvation is not our own doing. And so we can either compare ourselves with those around us, or we can be the most tender, humble people on the planet. We have no reason to boast. Grace is an unmerited gift.

#4. Good Works

The final result of grace we will consider is our good works. The next verse in the passage is Ephesians 2:10: "For we are his workmanship, created in Christ Jesus for good works, which God prepared beforehand, that we should walk in them."

You are not your own workmanship; you are His workmanship, created for good works. We are not given grace *because* of our works, but we are given works because of grace. Those are two very different things. Being prepared by grace for good works completely demolishes the idea of a cheap grace. It destroys a notion of Christianity that would preach grace upon grace, but never preach good works as a *product* of that grace. Taken as a whole, notice the arc of Paul's thought in these ten verses from Ephesians 2. In verses 1 and 2, it was spiritually dead people who walked in evil works. But in verse 10 it is spiritually alive people who walk in good works. The difference is *Sola Gratia*! As Christians saved by grace, it is our joy to abound in every good work.

> *We are not given grace because of our works, but we are given works because of grace. Those are two very different things.*

Second Corinthians 9:8 says, "And God is able to make all grace abound to you" (that's what has happened), "so that having all sufficiency in all things at all times" (that's what you have), "you may abound in every good work" (that's what you do). Abound in every good work. It's important to stress again that we abound in good works not to *earn* the grace that we've received, but *because* of the grace we've received. And so we serve people, love people, give our energy to ministry and discipleship, and readily speak the words of the gospel. In whatever circle of influence we are in, we show off God's goodness and grace.

There are countless other ways that grace is active in the life of the Christian, and we have only outlined four in this chapter! We have abundant life, the assurance of our salvation, humble hearts that cannot boast, and good works prepared for us to do.

May this grace be to us a source of joy and fuel our praise of God! The great doctrine of *Sola Gratia* should lead us to a place of reverent and humble awe. It should lead us to get on our knees in worship! May the Spirit, in grace and in power, cause these truths to solidify in our hearts.

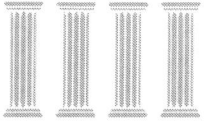

SOLA FIDE

(Faith Alone)

It's not an exaggeration to say that the doctrine of *Sola Fide,* or Faith Alone, is what radically changed the life of Martin Luther. It was this doctrine, which the Lord showed him in the Scriptures, that set him free from being deathly afraid of God and His justice. In fact, Luther's fear had been so great that he *hated* God—even though he was a monk. Thanks to God's mercy, Luther changed from being a man of fear and hate to being a man who joyfully ran into the arms of his heavenly Father. And it was all because of what Christ had done for him.

Scholars tell us that inside Luther's personal Bible he had these two words written: *"Sola Fide."* This was a constant reminder to him that he was not saved based on what he did or didn't do. His salvation was through faith in Christ and Christ alone—faith in what Jesus accomplished through His life, death, and resurrection on Luther's behalf.

The one goal of this chapter is to be very clear—even boringly predictable—in stating how exactly we are saved and made right with a holy God. At the very heart of how we are saved is the good news of the doctrine of *Sola Fide*. We're going to explore three questions pertaining to *Sola Fide*:

1.   What does "Faith Alone" mean?
2.   Where do we see it in Scripture?
3.   What difference should *Sola Fide* make in our everyday lives?

What Is Sola Fide?

Sola Fide, or "Faith Alone," is the biblical teaching that faith alone saves a person when that faith is placed in the sacrificial work of Christ alone.

It is vitally important to understand the inseparable nature of *Sola Fide* and *Solus Christus*, which we covered in chapter 2. We are saved by Christ alone, His righteousness alone, by His work alone—and *faith alone* is the way in which all the merits of Christ are credited to our account.

Another way of saying this is that *Sola Fide* teaches that we are declared righteous by God. We are justified. That's what justify means—to declare righteous. We are justified on the basis of our faith alone in Christ alone, *not* on the basis of our works. And this all happens because of grace alone (see chapter 3).

This word *justification* was a very important word to the Reformers. It was also a significant word to the biblical writers, the apostle Paul in particular. The word *justification* comes from the courtroom of the first century. Here's a picture of the term justification: imagine a courtroom setting as a trial is drawing to a close. The judge, having heard all the evidence, will pronounce the verdict. To justify a person in this context means to declare that he or she is *not guilty* in the eyes of the law.

How does that pertain to you and me and our justification before the Lord? A theologian named Anthony Carter hits the nail on the head. Let this soak in:

> Justification is God's declaration that sinners are in a right and acceptable relationship with him based solely on the person and work of Jesus Christ, the benefits of which are received by faith alone. It is the fact that those who were once enemies of God are now, through faith in Christ, friends and beloved. According to the Bible, this justification comes to those who believe through the blood of Christ. It comes to those who are "weak" and "ungodly." "Weak" speaks to our inability to save ourselves. It is the connotation that we are without strength and power. "Ungodly" speaks to our activity in opposition to the ways of God. It is the designation of sinners as impious, refusing to worship the God who created them, while living and loving contrary to his holy character and commands. Remarkably

. . . "Christ died for the ungodly." Here are five of the most heart-humbling, awe-inspiring, and joy-producing words you'll ever hear.[6]

Christ died for the ungodly!

We access the goodness of this gospel through *Sola Fide*. We are saved by an application of what theologians call "alien righteousness." That's a term that you, as a Christian, need to add to your vocabulary. When you think of an alien you probably think of a strange foreign being. But the word *alien* simply means "from another place." We are saved by righteousness that comes from another place. It doesn't come from within us as a result of anything we do or don't do; it comes completely from outside of ourselves, namely through the person and work of Jesus Christ alone.

We are saved by righteousness that comes from another place. It doesn't come from within us as a result of anything we do or don't do. . .

We've got to get this right. Christ's righteousness is imputed to us. It's ours when we repent of our sins and turn to Christ in faith alone. That's the good news of *Sola Fide*. We are saved by faith alone, and we are justified by faith alone.

Where Do We See *Sola Fide* in the Bible?

Is *Sola Fide* biblical? What we will see is that this doctrine of justification by faith alone actually helps to summarize what the Bible teaches over and over again regarding how sinners are saved. Literally hundreds of passages point to this great truth. So, yes, it's completely biblical! Let's unpack a few key verses.

Ephesians 2:8 — "For by grace you have been saved . . . "

The word that lies at the heart of all that is to follow in verses 8–9 is this word "grace." Although we've covered *Sola Gratia* in the last chapter, we observe again the inseparable nature of these doctrines. For by *grace* you have been saved! What a word! Paul is saying, "You want to look at the source of your salvation, Christian? The source of your salvation is the sheer grace of the God who made the heavens and the earth—the grace of God who made you and loves you and knows every hair on your head." In this particular context, grace is not just some general grace. Theologians make a distinction between the grace in Ephesians 2:8 and a different grace known as "common grace." If we're breathing and enjoying good things in life, such as food and loved ones, that's common grace—grace that is bestowed on all people because of the sheer kindness of God.

However, grace in the context of Ephesians 2 has to do very specifically with salvific grace. Grace that leads to salvation. Grace that takes the spiritually dead and brings them to life. Grace that removes the scales from spiritually blind eyes. Grace that's given to people who disregarded God but now causes them to see Jesus and His beauty, wanting nothing more than to worship Him and love Him with all that they are. It is the unmerited, unearned, undeserved favor of God shown to you that has caused your salvation. This is unbelievable grace!

Pastor and scholar Ligon Duncan puts it this way:

> God in saving you has showed you favor that you didn't deserve. In fact, he not only showed you favor that you didn't deserve, he showed you favor that you had positively disqualified yourself from by your rebellion against him, by your alienation, by your insurgency, by your walking according to the world and the flesh and the devil. And yet he lavished his favor on you. God, in his amazing grace, has saved you! As Romans 5:8 tells us, " . . . but God shows his love for us in that while we were still sinners, Christ died for us."[7]

What we must see here in this first part of Ephesians 2:8 is that our salvation begins and is sustained by the sovereign grace of our great God.

This leads to the second part of verse 8, where *Sola Fide* becomes explicit: "For by grace you have been saved *through faith* . . . " (emphasis mine). Salvation happens by grace *through faith*, and we must get the order right. Grace precedes our faith. This can be a bit complex, but here's what Paul is trying to communicate: *Though we receive salvation through faith, the cause of our faith in Christ is the grace of God.*

In the movie *Back to the Future*, there's a scene in which Michael J. Fox is on a skateboard, and he straps his backpack to the bumper of a moving car. Strapping your backpack to the bumper definitely seems like a good way to sit back and get somewhere more quickly.

Imagine you were him, and consider this question: What is the cause of your speed on the skateboard? What is the cause of your movement? Is it the backpack strap? No, it's not because of the strap. The strap has no power on its own; it is simply transferring the power of the car to you. The real cause of your speed is the car.

In a similar way, it is the grace of God that is the real power that makes us Christians. Faith is simply the strap. Faith is the channel of that grace. Here's the point: *Your salvation is not something that you have attained by your own doing.* It is something you have received by believing—by having faith in the Lord.

Faith is the channel of that grace.

Let's go a step further. Just as grace in Ephesians 2:8 is speaking of salvific grace, the faith that Paul is talking about is not just some generic faith—not just any kind of faith. The faith that Paul has in mind in Ephesians 2:8 is *saving faith* in Christ and Christ alone. The problem that so many people have is not with faith, it's with faith *in Christ*. Somebody may say, "I'm just not really a 'faith person.' I don't really have faith; that's not my thing." But of course that isn't true! The truth is that every person lives by radical faith in some cause, some person, or some thing. It just might not be Christ.

Let us not buy into this idea that some people have faith and some don't. The question is: Where is your faith placed? And what Paul is saying here is that saving faith is faith in Christ and in what He did through His life, His death, and His resurrection.

> *The truth is that every person lives by radical faith in some cause, some person, or some thing. It just might not be Christ.*

Paul concludes verse 8 and continues with verse 9: "For by grace you have been saved through faith. And this is not your own doing; it is the gift of God, not a result of works, so that no one may boast."

It's interesting Paul even writes verse 9. But, again, he doesn't want to leave any room for confusion. It's as if he's saying, "If I wasn't clear in verse 8, I just want you to know that we're not saved because of anything that we do or don't do. In any way." He wants to be clear on this for a reason because he has something very important to communicate: that everything we have and everything we do is ultimately for the glory of God and not self. That's the truth.

What Paul wants to make explicit is that if we take an ounce of credit for our salvation—the tiniest shred of credit—then our wicked hearts will quickly turn to arrogance and boasting. We may not say it out loud, but in our hearts we start to believe we're more holy than other people. More godly. That's what sin does; it twists us. What Paul is communicating is that when you are saved by grace alone through faith alone in Christ alone—you *will* boast. But you're going to boast in Christ! You're not going to boast in yourself.

At the heart of *Sola Fide* is a humbling of self and a glorifying of Christ. That's a good thing! That's a joyful thing. That's what we were made to do. Let's look next at Romans 4.

Romans 4:5 —*"And to the one who does not work but believes in him who justifies the ungodly, his faith is counted as righteousness."*

Here are five different ways this one verse teaches justification by faith alone:

The justified one does not work for their salvation.

Again, the word "justify" means "to declare righteous, to make one right with God." We do not work for our salvation.

The justified one believes.

There's belief at the heart of this. But the question remains: "Believes in *whom*?"

The justified one believes not in himself but in Him—in God, in Christ—who justifies.

The Christian doesn't have faith in himself, but in the Lord! He has faith in One so much greater.

The justified one confesses himself to be "ungodly."

To really lean into *Sola Fide* is to recognize that we need a savior, and we are not the Savior. In fact, in our natural state, we are ungodly; we have rebelled against God.

The justified one sees his faith credited to him as "righteousness."

We are justified and declared righteous by faith in Christ and His work alone.

Paul is so careful to be straightforward, and this verse is an example of his clarity. Let's consider our next verse:

Galatians 2:16 — " . . . *yet we know that a person is not justified by works of the law but through faith in Jesus Christ, so we also have believed in Christ Jesus, in order to be justified by faith in Christ and not by works of the law, because by works of the law no one will be justified."*

This couldn't be more clear! This verse encapsulates the whole letter to the Galatians—that we are not justified by works. We are justified by faith in Christ and His perfect work on our behalf.

Remember from our chapter on *Solus Christus* when Paul pointed out that if anyone could be saved by his or her works, it would be him? This is what he concludes in Philippians 3:8–9:

> Indeed, I count everything as loss because of the surpassing worth of knowing Christ Jesus my Lord. For his sake I have suffered the loss of all things and count them as rubbish, in order that I may gain Christ and be found in him, not having a righteousness of my own that comes from the law, but that which comes through faith in Christ, the righteousness from God that depends on faith . . .

Again, Paul's clarity is astounding. We're justified—we are declared righteous—not because of our perfect obedience to the law of God but through faith in Christ and His perfect obedience on our behalf.

Perhaps it's always been popular for people to believe that if they're "good," then they're going to heaven.

However, with that bold belief comes all sorts of questions. What makes a person good? Why is one person good and another person not good? This mind-set in our culture which seems so loving is completely false. In fact, biblically speaking, what we see is that *none* of us are good. We are truly dead in our sins. Yet there is one who was good, and that's Christ Jesus. It's only in Him and through Him that we find favor and acceptance with God.

This is what Paul is saying in Philippians 3:9, "not having a righteousness of my own." He might as well say, "I'm really not a good guy! This isn't a righteousness of my own that comes through the law but that which comes through faith in Christ."

Now understand this: the message of the gospel of Jesus Christ is not, "You must become a good person!" The message of the gospel of Jesus Christ is, "In faith, turn to Christ and be saved! Surrender to Christ who takes away your filthy sin and gives you His righteousness so that you might be right with God. Redeemed by God, justified in God, and saved by God and His grace." That's the gospel. That's *Sola Fide*. We cannot fix ourselves. You need the Lord to fix you, and so do I. We cannot justify ourselves before a holy God. We simply cannot. Only God can justify us and declare us righteous.

The Practical Realities of Sola Fide

What we believe about God as Christians—our theology—should shape everything about our lives. It should affect how we live. It should affect how we spend money. It should affect how we love people who are difficult to love. It should affect *everything*. This is true of the doctrine of *Sola Fide*. This is not just some intellectual doctrine that we learn for fun and can forget about later. This whole truth of salvation through faith alone should change everything.

The Reformers and the apostle Paul were not interested in simply teaching this doctrine to assure us of our salvation, though that's true. But, more so, this doctrine should affect the rest of our days on this earth until we are with the Lord face-to-face.

> *This whole truth of salvation through faith alone should change everything.*

Let's look at a few ways:

God's Pleasure, Not People's Approval

Because you are justified by faith alone, do you know that you are loved by God? You're adored by God. You're accepted by God. You're approved of by your heavenly Father, which means you don't need to spend the rest of your life trying to impress Him (or anyone else for that matter).

You don't need to spend your life paralyzed—and many people are absolutely paralyzed—by trying to please and win the approval of everybody else. This is reality: you will *never* win the approval of everyone else. There will always be people who are annoyed by you or who think you're not the greatest. It's hard to admit, but that's just how it is.

Thankfully, living as a justified son or daughter of the King empowers us to love other people from a place of security rather than insecurity. We have the power not to live in fear of other people but to love people and to encourage them—even when they think we're different, and even when they don't love us back. That's what the freedom of *Sola Fide* does. If you want to be free, stop trying to live your life for the approval of everybody else. Because you've been approved of by the only one that matters, and that's God the Father through His Son Jesus Christ.

Grace-Driven Life vs. Guilt-Driven Life

Many brothers and sisters in Christ live in a place of constant guilt and condemnation that is *not* of the Lord. It's a "guilt-driven lifecycle" versus a "grace-driven lifecycle."

In a guilt-driven lifecycle, the pattern goes like this: I sin, which leads me to a place of feeling really bad. That leads me to guilt and self-condemnation, which ultimately causes me to anxiously await God's punishment. This mentality births an ongoing lifestyle of fear, worry, and lack of assurance that God even loves me. And then, inevitably, I go back to the same old sin. Wash, rinse, repeat. There is no joy in that lifecycle.

For a lot of us, that's the life we're living even though we're Christians. That was the life Martin Luther lived before he understood *Sola Fide*. And you can see why he, while living in this guilt-driven cycle, eventually hated God!

How *Sola Fide* changes everything! This is a grace-driven lifecycle: Although I hate it, I still sin. This leads me to a place of feeling really bad. But I repent, and that is where things begin to change. I'm no longer living by guilt and growing more and more fearful as I await punishment from God. When I truly understand *Sola Fide* and the grace of God, after repenting, I *celebrate* that Christ Jesus took my punishment upon Himself! I have faith that He took *all* my sin! Am I worthy of that substitution? NO! I am not worthy of it. But I am so thankful that Jesus Christ died in my place.

You know where this lifecycle leads? Joy in the Lord! Joy in my justification, which frees me to worship God because He approved of me in Christ. Wash, rinse, repeat. We preach to ourselves the truths of justification, being confident in what Jesus has done for us. Satan wants us to be fearful, but the Word of God tells us to remember the promises of what He's done.

These are two completely different ways to live the Christian life. Some of us are living a guilt-driven life, but the good news is that Jesus died that you might no longer live your life that way. This doctrine of *Sola Fide* frees us to live from a place of grace because of who we now are as Christians. Our identity is in Christ. The guilt-driven narrative is fueled by lies! But the grace-driven narrative is fueled by freedom in Christ.

Isn't that good news?!

Unity with Other Believers

In his letters to both the Romans and the Galatians, Paul wants his readers to see that both Jewish Christians and Gentile Christians are united because of this doctrine. Every person is saved and justified the same way—through faith. "For all have sinned and fall short of the glory of God, and are justified by his grace as a gift, through the redemption that is in Christ Jesus, whom God put forward as a propitiation by his blood, to be received by faith . . . . For we hold that one is justified by faith apart from works of the law" (Romans 3:23–25, 28).

This rings true today! *Sola Fide* frees us to celebrate the unity that we have as Christians. There's a shallower unity out there that people want to accept simply for being part of the human race. But we have something that goes so much deeper for all of eternity. Brothers and sisters are unified because we have been saved by grace through faith in Christ alone. He is our great unifier.

How does this work practically in the local church? Even though—or even *because*—we make different amounts of money, live in different neighborhoods, look different, sound different, and come from different backgrounds, we celebrate our unity! Here's a unifying truth about heaven: it's not going to be a whole bunch of people that look like me. It's going to be a beautiful tapestry of every tribe and tongue and nation praising Jesus. It'll be more wonderful than we can imagine.

> *Brothers and sisters are unified because we have been saved by grace through faith in Christ alone. He is our great unifier.*

And when Jesus prays things like, "Father, Your will be done on earth as it is in heaven," part of His desire is for His followers to be a unified body *here and now*. Certainly, we are different from each other. Yet we are saved by the same Christ in the same way, by grace through faith. That's unity! Don't you want to be a part of that church? That's the kind of church for which Jesus died.

Good Works for the Glory of God

Some will argue against *Sola Fide.* They will say, "If you Protestants teach this doctrine, then you're just teaching people to only believe, and then live their lives however they want. You're giving them license to live in sin." But clearly, that argument is a misunderstanding of *Sola Fide*—and it's a misrepresentation of what the Bible teaches. Yes, *Sola Fide* teaches that we are saved by grace alone through faith alone, but when we are saved through that faith, it leads to a life of surrender. It leads to a life of loving others. It leads to a life of good works. We discussed this in the last chapter, but it should be repeated. The difference is that we no longer do good works for our glory, but we do good works for the glory of God.

That's what *Sola Fide* does. Don't buy for a second the argument that you have to do something to earn your salvation. But undoubtedly that salvation results in a different kind of life—a life that loves to follow the Word of God and loves to love God and people. It's a life of intentional obedience.

The book of James talks about this; James clearly believed in *Sola Fide.* But what he is emphasizing in his letter is that faith results in a life that cares about others— a life that results in good works.

> What good is it, my brothers, if someone says he has faith but does not have works? Can that faith save him? If a

brother or sister is poorly clothed and lacking in daily food, and one of you says to them, "Go in peace, be warmed and filled," without giving them the things needed for the body, what good is that? So also faith by itself, if it does not have works, is dead. (James 2:14–17)

James is right on, and here is his point: "If you tell me that you love Jesus, but you don't love people or care about the poor, I question whether you really love Jesus." It's an indictment against easy believism. For those who have been saved by Christ, through faith alone, we are new creations in Him. Of course, we're still fighting our sin. But our *affections* have changed. Our *identity* has changed. We desire the things of God now, and those changed desires bear fruit through good works.

In light of all that the biblical writers have put forth in these selected Scriptures, the question that they would ask of each one of us today is this: Have you put your faith *in* Christ alone, that you might be justified *through* Christ alone? The only way that sinful men and women can be made right with God—declared righteous before a perfect and holy God—is through that kind of faith in Christ alone.

Romans 3:22 says it this way, "the righteousness of God through faith in Jesus Christ for all who believe."

Will we believe in Christ? Will we trust in Him? Will we place our faith in Him and be saved?

For those of us who have surrendered to Christ and who can quite frankly teach these very things to others, the question for us is: Are you living as a justified son or daughter of the King? You may believe this, even be able to preach it, but are you living by guilt or by grace?

Life on Mission

As a final note, let's consider the missional implication of *Sola Fide*. This good news is what people all throughout our world are dying to hear. The glory of this doctrine isn't just good news for those of us who know already know Christ. We are daily surrounded by people who are going to hell and need to know that they too can be saved by grace alone, through faith alone, in Christ alone. And we have been called to share that good news with the world—to the ends of the earth. Will we go? May the Lord give us the strength and courage to share the good news of *Sola Fide* with great love and compassion, from our doorsteps to the ends of the earth.

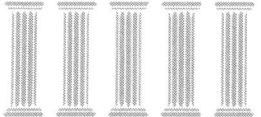

SOLA DEO GLORIA

(The Glory of God Alone)

As we near the end of this book, let's consider how the five *Solas* fit together. Steven Lawson paints a picture of the five *Solas* fitting together in a unique way.[8] Imagine the *Solas* as a building. The foundation of this building is *Sola Scriptura*. This foundation, which must be solid, holds that the Bible alone is our authority on all matters of faith, practice, and life. On this foundation we have these next three pillars: *Sola Gratia, Sola Fide,* and *Solus Christus.* These pillars are deeply cemented into the foundation of *Sola Scriptura*. They are the outflow of what the Scriptures teach.

The building metaphor is apt because it shows us what happens if there is a crack in the foundation. If *Sola Scriptura* is jeopardized, you can imagine what begins to happen to the pillars of Grace Alone, Faith Alone, and Christ Alone. If the crack begins to spread and grow in the foundation, then the pillars themselves begin to crumble.

Sadly, that is what has happened throughout the history of the church at different times and in different denominations or local congregations. That is what has happened in many parachurch ministries and seminaries. The Scriptures are compromised, and it invariably leads to a view that the Bible is insufficient. And if the Bible is insufficient, then the clarity of salvation through Grace Alone, Faith Alone, and in Christ Alone becomes distorted.

This is why we stand with the Reformers when we talk about salvation. We show *from the Bible* how God saves us. And here's the good news: when the foundation of Scripture Alone remains solid, then the pillars of Grace Alone, Faith Alone, and Christ Alone are firm on that foundation.

But the building isn't quite complete, and that is the subject of this chapter. The result of a firm scriptural foundation and its accompanying doctrines is the overarching pinnacle of the building: *Soli Deo Gloria.* For the Glory of God Alone.

When we understand Scripture rightly, we see clearly that it teaches we're saved by grace alone through faith alone in Christ alone, and that naturally leads to the glory of God alone. These doctrines produce Christians who are so overwhelmed by the loving grace of Jesus that we can't help but live for the glory of God. That's the kind of church that Jesus died for us to be because living and dying for the glory of God was His own mission.

In the previous chapters, we have sought to answer the question of how we are saved. In this chapter, we want to be just as clear in answering the question of *why* we are saved. Why is *anyone* saved? Have you ever wondered that? The answer is as simple as it is profound: we are saved

When we understand Scripture rightly, we see clearly that it teaches we're saved by grace alone through faith alone in Christ alone, and that naturally leads to the glory of God alone.

for the glory of God alone. *Soli Deo Gloria*. It's a beautiful doctrine. As you read this chapter, may you worship! We have a great salvation and a great God to glorify!

Defining Soli Deo Gloria

Soli Deo Gloria means, "God alone deserves all glory, honor, and praise—particularly in His work of saving sinners by grace alone through faith alone in Christ alone." Let's zero in on the first part of this definition. We've got to get this right—that God alone deserves all glory, honor, and praise.

The word "glory" comes from the Greek word *doxa*, which literally means "glory" or "praise." To glory in something means to honor or praise something because of its supreme value and significance—which is only legitimate if that something is *actually* glorious. We can glory in something that isn't deserving of praise. And if we do it at the level of the heart, then we've ventured into idolatry.

But to glorify God is fundamentally different. We aren't ascribing glory to something that isn't glorious. We are *recognizing* Him as He is: the glorious One. Our praise doesn't make Him glorious—we are simply savoring Him for who He is. Celebrating Him as majestic, worthy of worship, deserving of all praise and adoration.

This is what David means when he writes in 1 Chronicles 16:28–29, "Ascribe to the LORD glory and strength . . . the glory due his name." He is already worthy of glory. In fact, He *alone* is worthy of glory.

Look at your own life. I'm guessing at some point you have wondered, *Why in the world am I alive? Why am I on this earth? What is the point of this whole thing?* The answer to that age-old existential question is answered in *Soli Deo Gloria!* We exist as human beings to bring glory to God.

The Westminster Shorter Catechism addresses it this way:

> Question: What is the chief end of man?
> Answer: The chief end of man is to glorify God and enjoy Him forever.

That is our purpose. This is why we're miserable when we seek to glorify ourselves and our jobs, our money, our stuff, our kids, sports, or any number of less-than-glorious things. Life is found when we live for God's glory and enjoy Him forever.

Here's something we may not think about very often: God *desires* to be glorified. The God of the heavens and the earth wants to be glorified. In fact, He is zealous for His glory. When this self-glorifying shows up in people, we call it

> *This is why we're miserable when we seek to glorify ourselves and our jobs, our money, our stuff, our kids, sports, or any number of less-than-glorious things.*

arrogance. Self-centeredness. Self-promotion. We are naturally repulsed by it.

But it's a really good thing when it comes to God. God is passionate about His own glory, and it would be wrong of Him to want anything or anyone *other* than Himself to receive that glory. Why? Because He *is* the most glorious thing. Human beings are not inherently worthy of glory. But our Maker is! Here is a sampling of some verses in the Scriptures that speak to God being passionate about His glory:

- Isaiah 43:6–7 —"Bring my sons from afar and my daughters from the end of the earth, everyone who is called by my name, whom I created for my glory . . . "
- Matthew 5:16 —"In the same way, let your light shine before others, so that they may see your good works and give glory to your Father who is in heaven."
- Romans 15:7 —"Therefore welcome one another as Christ has welcomed you, for the glory of God."
- 1 Peter 4:11 —". . . whoever serves, [let him do it] as one who serves by the strength which God supplies— in order that in everything God may be glorified through Jesus Christ. To him belong glory and dominion forever and ever. Amen."
- Habakkuk 2:14 —"For the earth will be filled with the knowledge of the glory of the LORD as the waters cover the sea."
- 1 Corinthians 10:31 —"So, whether you eat or drink, or whatever you do, do all to the glory of God."

Our existence, our good works, our fellowship, our serving of others and the world around us—all of it centered upon the glory of God.

We could go on and on and on, but the Bible makes it obvious that God alone deserves the glory, and it should be our joy to glorify Him. We've got to get that. That's part one of our definition of *Soli Deo Gloria*: "God alone deserves all glory, honor, and praise . . . "

This statement seems to be enough in and of itself. But it's the second part of the definition where we must really focus: " . . . particularly in His work of saving sinners by grace alone, through faith alone, in Christ alone."

This second half of the definition gets to the heart of *Soli Deo Gloria*. We're not just talking about God deserving glory—though that's true! What we're speaking of specifically in the culmination of the five *Solas* is that God alone deserves the glory in our salvation. As the Reformers saw it, God deserves all the glory in our salvation because, from beginning to end, our salvation is a gift from Him. Martin Luther put it this way:

> God has surely promised His grace to the humbled—that is, to those who mourn over and despair of themselves. But a man cannot be thoroughly humbled till he realizes that his salvation is utterly beyond his own powers, counsels, efforts, will and works, and depends absolutely on the will, counsel, pleasure and work of Another—God alone.[9]

This is amazing grace! Luther and the other Reformers taught so clearly that God alone is glorified in our salvation because it is God alone who was pleased to save us, God alone who willed it, and God alone who worked it.

Let's look at this doctrine in Paul's letter to the Corinthians. The apostle Paul wrote to the church in Corinth, "And because of him you are in Christ Jesus, who became to us wisdom from God, righteousness and sanctification and redemption, so that, as it is written, 'Let the one who boasts, boast in the Lord'" (1 Corinthians 1:30–31).

The entire first chapter of 1 Corinthians culminates in these last two verses. What Paul wants his readers to see—and what he wants us to see—is that our salvation is completely and utterly dependent on God *by His grace* and *for His glory.*

Like the Reformers after him, Paul wants us to see that our salvation is 100 percent of God. As we've noted, some would teach falsely that our salvation is 50 percent God's doing and 50 percent our doing. Or, if we want to be generous, 90 percent God's doing and 10 percent our doing. Or even 99 percent God's doing and 1 percent our doing! But the unbelievable news of the Christian gospel is that salvation is 100 percent God. If we even took a tiny fraction of 1 percent, do you know where that would lead? To boasting. To stealing glory that only belongs to God.

We can never say with integrity: "Look what I've done!" According to the Scriptures, we were dead in our sins. Dead! Dead people don't contribute to anything, let alone their salvation! Remember Ephesians 2 from our

> *. If we even took a tiny fraction of 1 percent, do you know where that would lead? To boasting. To stealing glory that only belongs to God.*

chapter on *Sola Gratia?* We needed to be reborn by the Spirit of God. Our salvation is 100 percent God, and this is good news for sinners like us!

We need to understand a little bit about the Corinthians, the audience to whom Paul is writing here. There had been a time in which they had come to Christ, and, while they were new Christians, they were soft toward God. They were teachable. They were humble. They put themselves under the Word of God willingly and joyfully. They were sponges, soaking up the truth about Christ, like the Bereans from chapter 1. That's true of a lot of new Christians. The problem is that over time these Corinthians began to think pretty highly of themselves. They drifted. Sadly, this also happens in many churches today. We move from a place of dependence—a place of humility, a place of eagerness to give God glory—to a place of self-sufficiency. Paul is writing to these Corinthians to remind them of the truth that they knew but needed reinforced—that they are what they are by the grace of God.

Perhaps each of us on some level need this truth reinforced in our hearts, that we might ascribe more glory to God alone!

Look again at the first part of 1 Corinthians 1:30: "And because of him you are in Christ Jesus . . . " If you are a Christian today, there is only one reason: it's because of *Him*. The fact that we have been born again and are now united to Christ is because of God's will, God's grace, God's plan. That's what Paul is reminding these Corinthians because they had forgotten! We are saved solely because of God's doing, not our own. It's not like we fly into heaven with God as one wing of the plane, and we've got the other wing of the plane. God *is* the plane, and by His grace He puts us on it.

Yes, the Bible is clear that we need to respond in faith to the gracious work of God. We covered this in our chapter on *Sola Fide.* We are absolutely responsible to put our faith and trust in the gospel of Jesus Christ. Romans 10:9–10 states, "If you confess with your mouth that Jesus is Lord and believe in your heart that God raised him from the dead, you will be saved. For with the heart one believes and is justified, and with the mouth one confesses and is saved."

If you are not a Christian, this is a call to action! Confess Jesus as Lord, put your faith in Him, and be saved! That's the invitation of Christ. But even *Sola Fide* is a product of *Sola Gratia.* That is what Paul means in verse 30 when he says, "and because of him you are in Christ Jesus." *Sola Fide* and *Sola Gratia* must always lead us to *Soli Deo Gloria!*

This is the amazing grace that John Newton, who wrote the hymn "Amazing Grace," had in mind when he looked into the Word of God. He saw the same thing we're looking at in this chapter, and he was blown away that he was saved not because he was a good guy or because he was a good rule-follower, but solely because of the grace of God in Christ. That should lead us to sing as it led Newton to sing!

The Wisdom of God

Paul continues in 1 Corinthians 1:30, " . . . who became to us wisdom from God, righteousness and sanctification and redemption . . . " Because of God, you are in Christ Jesus. And for the Christian, Jesus became to us four things: *wisdom from God, righteousness, sanctification, and redemption*. How do we understand verse 30? "Wisdom from God" is a key phrase here. This phrase stands alone, so we need to look at it separately. Because what flows out of this wisdom from God are three benefits: righteousness, sanctification, and redemption.

What exactly is this wisdom from God? Some would say this wisdom from God has to do with us literally receiving wisdom or insight from God, at the point of salvation. The verse may very well convey that meaning. When the Lord gives us new life in Him—when we are saved—we have access to godly wisdom from above. But there's more to it than that.

Steven Lawson rightly points out that the phrase "wisdom from God" in 1 Corinthians 1 is in other verses used synonymously with the gospel. It's used interchangeably with the salvation that comes from God through Christ alone.[10] Here are some examples:

1. In verse 18, this wisdom from God is the word of the cross.
2. In verse 21, this wisdom from God is the message to save.
3. In verse 23, this wisdom from God is Christ crucified.
4. In verse 24, this wisdom from God is the power from God and the wisdom from God in the cross.

Here's the point: the greatest display of the wisdom of God is in the death of Christ for sinners, in which God is both just and the justifier. God displays His perfect holiness and, at the same time, displays His perfect grace for the salvation of broken sinners.

This is the genius plan of salvation! We would have never come up with this. In the gospel—in Christ crucified, in our salvation—we see the perfect wisdom of God. That is what Paul is saying.

The outflow of this wisdom is threefold. Verse 30 concludes: " . . . who became to us wisdom from God, righteousness and sanctification and redemption . . . " Christ Jesus became to us righteousness, became to us sanctification, and became to us redemption. Let's look at each of these briefly.

Righteousness

What is righteousness? As previously mentioned, righteousness means that not only are we legally declared "not guilty," but we also now have a *positive* righteousness, known as an "alien righteousness." Recall from chapter 4 that alien means "from another place." Could our good deeds in any way conjure up a righteousness that makes us acceptable to God? No, this alien righteousness could only come through the perfect life, death, and resurrection of Jesus Christ. Jesus became for us righteousness.

Sanctification

Sanctification literally means to be set apart or to be washed or to be made holy. It speaks of our growth in holiness and our maturing in godliness and Christlikeness. But sanctification doesn't happen when we look inward. Being made holy happens as we look to Christ and as we abide in Him. Christ is the one who sanctifies us by the Spirit. *He* makes us holy. We don't make ourselves holy. He helps us to die to the things of this world so we might live lives of purity for His glory. That's what Paul means in verse 30 when he says that Jesus became for us sanctification.

Redemption

Redemption means purchasing or setting someone free from captivity or slavery by paying a price. The supreme Old Testament example is the exodus. God redeems the nation of Israel, His chosen people, from slavery in Egypt.

When we study this word *redemption* throughout Scripture, here's what we see: redeeming a person in the Bible always involves paying a price referred to as a ransom. In redeeming us, in setting us free from the bondage of sin, God had to pay a price. So, the question some may ask is, "How did He do this? Was it money? Was it gold and silver? How did He pay the price for our sin against Himself?"

God the Father paid the price through the shedding of His precious Son's blood on the cross for us. The perfect sacrifice was made so that our sins might be covered and so that we might be reconciled to God—that we might be redeemed. Jesus paid our debt.

When we sing the song "Jesus Paid It All," we mean it! Many people need to hear this today. Because they might believe they paid for at least part of their sin. But when Jesus died on the cross, He died for *all* of your sins—past, present, and future. Brother and sister in Christ, you are redeemed through the blood of Jesus. You are declared righteous, and you are being sanctified by the grace of God alone.

This is all God! This is all His love! All His grace! All His mercy for sinners. Verse 30, although short, is a theologically-packed verse. Paul is making the point that our salvation is all of God and not of us. Jesus became for us wisdom from God, righteousness, sanctification, and redemption.

All of this leads to the question . . . why?

Why Are We Saved?

Why did God save you, Christian? Have you ever asked that? Are you ever amazed by that? Going a step further, why did He choose to save you in the way that He did? Why *Solus Christus, Sola Gratia, Sola Fide*? He could've made us work for it—He is God, after all. But thankfully, He isn't like that!

Paul gives us the answer in verse 31: " . . . so that, as it is written, 'Let the one who boasts, boast in the Lord.'" Why did God save us the way that He did? That we might boast in *Him!* That we might praise *Him!* That we might glorify *Him* and that He would get all the

Why did God save us the way that He did? That we might boast in Him!

glory that He deserves. This is what *Soli Deo Gloria* is all about—He alone is worthy of all the glory.

Now let's look at 1 Corinthians 1:26. I want us to see the context of verses 30 and 31 in order to add a little more color to this picture. Remember the context: Paul is writing to these Corinthians who have become a little self-absorbed. They've forgotten about the grace of God. They have begun to lean on worldly wisdom instead of godly wisdom.

In 1 Corinthians 1:26 he begins: "For consider your calling, brothers [and sisters] . . . " What does Paul mean when he uses the word "calling"? He means God is calling them literally *to* Himself. When you became a Christian, He called to *you*. You didn't call to Him; He called to you. You responded. Paul is saying, "Remember when God called you? Remember when you were in that place? You had no interest in Him, but He called you." Paul goes on in verses 27-31:

> . . . not many of you were wise according to worldly standards, not many were powerful, not many were of noble birth. But God chose what is foolish in the world to shame the wise; God chose what is weak in the world to shame the strong; God chose what is low and despised in the world, even things that are not, to bring to nothing things that are, so that no human being might boast in the presence of God. And because of him you are in Christ Jesus, who became to us wisdom from God, righteousness and sanctification and redemption, so that, as it is written, "Let the one who boasts, boast in the Lord.

Consider these verses as well:

Thus says the LORD: "Let not the wise man boast in his wisdom, let not the mighty man boast in his might, let not the rich man boast in his riches, but let him who boasts boast in this, that he understands and knows me, that I am the LORD who practices steadfast love, justice, and righteousness in the earth. For in these things I delight, declares the LORD." (Jeremiah 9:23–24)

For by grace you have been saved through faith. And this is not your own doing; it is the gift of God, not a result of works, so that no one may boast. (Ephesians 2:8–9)

Again, as human beings, we are created to boast, but not in ourselves or any other thing or person. We are created and wired to ultimately boast in the Lord. Through Jesus, we have been saved and redeemed that we might actually do this! How can we not? We *must* boast in the Lord. If you are a new creation, you can't help it!

This may be confusing to some of us, because throughout our sanctification process we can still feel so attracted to the things of the world. But we know where real freedom and joy and life is found: in living for the glory of God. We increasingly become less, He becomes more. We forget ourselves, that He might be remembered. We shine the spotlight on Him, not on ourselves. We were made for this and saved for this: to boast in the Lord, glorifying and enjoying Him forever!

The Practical Realities of *Soli Deo Gloria*

How do we boast in the Lord? We boast in the Lord through our lips and through our lives in a million different ways. Here are just a few:

#1. *We Boast in the Lord in Our Songs*

When nobody else is around, and you look like a crazy fool in your car as you sing along to God-centered worship music, He is glorified! "Lord, I sing praises to Your name. You're so good! You're so kind!"

#2. *We Boast the Lord in Our Prayers*

We say, "Oh God, You are majestic. You are mighty. You are wonderful. You are my God." How many of the Psalms we can turn to for examples!

#3. *We Boast in the Lord in Our Witness*

As we share the good news of salvation in Christ, as we proclaim this wisdom from God, He is glorified. And by His power, He is glorified as people respond in faith and He saves and redeems sinners!

#4. We Boast in the Lord in Our Obedience

Our disobedience cannot boast in God. Obeying Him is not a burden. It's a joy! Unfortunately, sometimes we get fearful. We live in a day and age in which even Bible-believing Christians believe that a life of holiness is outdated. No! Living a

As we share the good news of salvation in Christ, as we proclaim this wisdom from God, He is glorified.

holy life brings pleasure to our God! Fighting sin and pursuing righteousness by the grace and power of God is where life is found.

Are you walking in obedience, or are you walking in disobedience? The Lord wants to forgive you. The Lord wants to work in you. The Lord wants you to live for His glory. Maybe that begins right now by saying, "God, I need to confess. I'm tired of holding on to my sin. I'm tired of living this way." I don't have to prove to you that your sin makes you miserable. And God is saying, "Bring it to Me. Bring it to Me so I can free you to live for My glory, and so you can boast in Me."

#5. We Boast in the Lord in Our Enjoyment

God wants us to enjoy Him. Enjoying God—that's odd for some of us. But enjoying God brings glory to God, as we saw in the Westminster Catechism. John Piper puts it this way: "God is most glorified in us when we are most satisfied in Him."[11] That is true. Those two things are not at odds. We boast in Him in our lives when we enjoy Him and treasure Him above all other things.

We boast in Him in our lives when we enjoy Him and treasure Him above all other things.

#6. We Boast in the Lord in Our Trust

Trust in ourselves, trust in the world, trust in others—all of these will leave us wanting. As Christians, we boast in the Lord when we trust in the Lord. We trust in His revealed Word. We trust in His promises. In doing so, what we are saying time and time again is, "Lord, there is no one but You. Glorify Yourself through me."

Closing Thoughts

Fittingly, from God's Word comes the culmination of this book. Memorize this verse and ask your family and friends to memorize it. This verse shouts out everything that we've been looking at in the five *Solas,* clearly pointing all the praise to the only One who is worthy of it:

> Not to us, O LORD, not to us, but to your name give glory, for the sake of your steadfast love and your faithfulness! (Psalm 115:1)

Our prayer is that in being reminded of these truths your soul has again been set aflame for the awe-inspiring, praise-inducing, pride-shattering, God-glorifying realities of the five *Solas.* May these doctrines for which the Reformers fought produce in us such a wonder at the glories of our salvation that our worship of God reaches new heights and depths! And what a salvation it is: rooted in Scripture Alone, through Faith Alone, by Grace Alone, in Christ Alone, and for the Glory of God Alone! Amen.

NOTES

[1] Second Council of the Vatican (November 18, 1965); Chapter II, no. 9; http://www.vatican.va/archive/hist_councils/ii_vatican_council/documents/vat-ii_const_19651118_dei-verbum_en.html.

[2] "Scripture and Plain Reason," *Grace to You,* accessed June 12, 2018, https://www.gty.org/library/articles/A243/scripture-and-plain-reason

[3] Westminster Confession of Faith (1647); Chapter 1.6; http://www.reformation21.org/confession/2013/01/chapter-16.php.

[4] Steven J. Lawson, "The Sufficiency of Scripture in Expository Preaching," *Expositor Magazine*, Sept/Oct 2014, 10.

[5] Steven J. Lawson, "General Session 10" (Sermon delivered at the Inerrancy Summit, Sun Valley, CA, March 3-8, 2015), https://www.gracechurch.org/sermons/10916?AspxAutoDetectCookieSupport=1.

[6] Anthony Carter, "Justified by His Blood," *Tabletalk Magazine* (April 1, 2011), https://www.ligonier.org/learn/articles/justified-his-blood/.

[7] Dr. J. Ligon Duncan, III, "Saved From, By, For What," (Sermon, First Presbyterian Church, Jacksonville, MS, October 16, 2005),

https://www.fpcjackson.org/resource-library/sermons/saved-from-by-for-what.

[8] Steven Lawson, "Solus Christus" (Sermon, One Passion Ministries, Dallas, TX, May 31, 2015), https://www.sermonaudio.com/sermoninfo.asp?m=t&s=8415163126.

[9] Martin Luther, *The Bondage of the Will* (Grand Rapids: Fleming H. Revell, 1992), 40.

[10] Steven Lawson, "Solus Christus," (Sermon, One Passion Ministries, Dallas, TX, May 31, 2015), https://www.sermonaudio.com/sermoninfo.asp?m=t&s=8415163126.

[11] Piper, John. *Desiring God, Revised Edition: Meditations of a Christian Hedonist* (Colorado Springs, CO: Waterbrook Multnomah, 2011) Kindle Edition, Location 73.

"Mark Hallock is not only passionate about seeing more shepherd preachers fill our pulpits, he is one who seeks to live it out in his own life and ministry."

Alexander Strauch, Author of *Biblical Eldership* and *Leading with Love*

What kind of preachers do our churches need now?

Welcome to the Family is an insider's look into the Calvary Family of Churches (CFC)—its core values and doctrines are on full display as multiple authors ranging from church pastors and members to planters and replanters come together to form a united vision for the church. Readers will find the contents to be thought-provoking and informative, helping those curious about the CFC to understand **(and perhaps join)** the vision and hope of the movement.

EDITED BY
MARK HALLOCK

acomapress.org

ACOMA PRESS

Acoma Press exists to make Jesus non-ignorable by equipping and encouraging churches through gospel-centered resources.

Toward this end, each purchase of an Acoma Press resource serves to catalyze disciple-making and to equip leaders in God's Church. In fact, a portion of your purchase goes directly to funding planting and replanting efforts in North America and beyond. To see more of our current resources, visit us at *acomapress.org*.

Thank you.

54757734R00065

Made in the USA
Columbia, SC
06 April 2019